Our Sunday Best

A *For Better or For Worse*® Sunday Collection
by Lynn Johnston

Andrews, McMeel & Parker
A Universal Press Syndicate Company
Kansas City · New York

ISBN: 0-8362-2057-9

Library of Congress Catalog Card Number: 84-81551

3

For Better or For Worse

By Lynn Johnston

WHERE ARE YOU GOING, MOM?

TO A MAKE-UP DEMONSTRATION.

DO YOU THINK IT'LL HELP?

GOOD EVENING, LADIES! — WELCOME TO THE WORLD OF "SKIN GOODNESS MULTI-PHASE NEW-YOUTH CLINIC!"

ALL WASHED? NOW WE APPLY PHASE 1 GRAPE AND AVOCADO MOISTURE TONIC!

AFTER OUR PHASE 2 EYEBAG TENDERIZER, LET'S EXPERIMENT WITH OUR "LOW TIDE TONER!"

WE'LL CAMOUFLAGE THOSE TELL-TALE WRINKLES WITH THE PHASE 3 PRIMER COAT!

BE MORE FLIPPANT WITH YOUR WHIPPED SHADOW DELIGHT, MRS. PATTERSON!

LEARN ANYTHING AT YOUR MAKE-UP PARTY, ELLY?

YEAH.

I'VE GOT ALLERGIES.

5

6

For Better or For Worse
By Lynn Johnston

14

For Better or For Worse
By Lynn Johnston

AAAGH!

AAGH!!! NOT AGAIN!

STUPID, DUMB, CRUMMY CRASH!!

NO! AAH! I DON'T WANNA GO TO BED! WAAAH!!

MOM? AREN'T YOU GONNA KISS ME GOODNIGHT?

TO TELL YOU THE TRUTH, MIKE, WHEN YOU ACT LIKE THAT.... I JUST DON'T FEEL LIKE KISSING YOU AT ALL!

BUT, MOM.... THAT'S WHEN I NEED IT MOST!

17

18

For Better or For Worse

By Lynn Johnston

19

For Better or For Worse
By Lynn Johnston

MOM ... ELIZABETH JUST WENT OUTSIDE.

MMPHHH

SHE'S GOT HER RED UMBRELLA...

MMMM

AND SHE'S WEARING HER NEW RED BOOTS.

HMZZZz

— AND NOTHING ELSE.

I LIKE SAVING THE BEST FOR LAST.

For Better or For Worse
By Lynn Johnston

RRING!!

GZMF?

RRING!

HMMMH...

RRINGG!

SNORT...UH?

HU...HULLO?

HI, BABY,... HEH, HEH, PANT, WHEEZE...

WHAT?

HI, BABY... BREEEATHE, WHEEZE, PANT, HUFFF, SNICKER

HMPH? I DON'T UNNERSTAN'...

I SAID HI, BABY! WHEEZE, PANT! HUFF..HUFF!

SAY THAT AGAIN?

OH FOR *!@☆ SAKE, LADY— FORGET IT!!! (CLICK)

WHAT WAS THAT?

MY FIRST OBSCENE PHONE CALL...

—AND I MISSED IT.

28

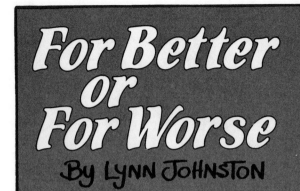

For Better or For Worse
By Lynn Johnston

MMMMM
MFF
MFF MFF

POP!

KEEP SUCKING YOUR THUMB LIKE THAT, LIZZIE – AND IT'LL FALL OFF!

YEAH! – AN' KNOW WHAT? IF YOU PRESS YOUR BELLY BUTTON, YOUR LEGS WILL FALL OFF!

BLPPFFT!

AN' IF YOU STICK OUT YOUR TONGUE TOO FAR – YOUR EARS WILL FALL OFF!!

WAAAAH!

ELIZABETH! WHAT IS THE MATTER?

I FALLING APART!!!

For Better or For Worse
By Lynn Johnston

HOLY COW! - ANOTHER BATCH OF CHRISTMAS CARDS!

PFLADDAP!

I WANNA SEE! ME SEE!

HMMM .... ALMA, O.K., JESSIE, HELEN BINKS, MARJ AND BERNARD, NANCY AND JIM, FRED AND MAUREEN, CHECK...

WHATCHA DOIN', MOM?

I'M CHECKING OFF PEOPLE WHO SEND ME CARDS.

IF I SEND A CARD - THEN DON'T GET ONE BACK, I CROSS THOSE PEOPLE OFF MY LIST.

"SCRIBBLE" DRAW..

CHRISTMAS CARDS - FOR ME? HOW NICE!

WE WANTED TO STAY ON YOUR LIST.

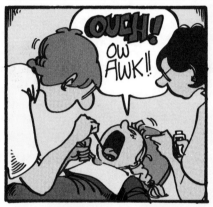

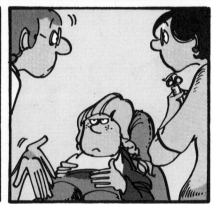

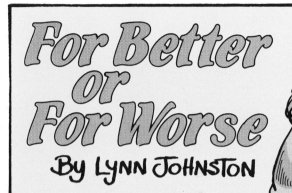

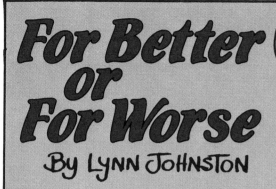

For Better or For Worse

By Lynn Johnston

JOHN! WHAT HAVE YOU DONE?!!

I GOT A HAIRCUT.

BUT... IT'S SO SHORT! — IT LOOKS AWFUL!!

YEAH?-WELL, THE BARBER AND I GOT TO TALKING-AND THE MORE WE TALKED, THE MORE HE CUT!

AAAGH! — I CAN'T STAND IT!!-HOW COULD YOU DO THIS TO ME?!!

IT'LL GROW BACK. BESIDES-YOU DIDN'T MARRY ME FOR MY LOOKS... YOU MARRIED ME FOR MY GREAT PERSONALITY!!

BRAAK!

....SO MUCH FOR PERSONALITY.

For Better or For Worse

By Lynn Johnston

JOHN, I WISH YOU WOULDN'T REFER TO YOUR STAFF AS "YOUR GIRLS."

OH?

WELL... AREN'T THEY?

I TOOK JEAN OUT FOR LUNCH TODAY, ELLY... AND WE HAD A LONG TALK.

SHE'S BEEN A LITTLE DEPRESSED LATELY, SO I THOUGHT I'D FIND OUT WHY.

WE DISCUSSED HER CHILDHOOD, HER FAMILY, HER FEELINGS ABOUT HER JOB WITH ME AT THE CLINIC.

SHE TOLD ME ABOUT HER MARRIAGE, HER WORRIES, HOW SHE FEELS ABOUT HERSELF...

WHAT'S THE MATTER?

NOTHING.

DON'T YOU THINK IT'S GOOD THAT I HAVE THESE IN-DEPTH, PERSONAL TALKS WITH THE PEOPLE I WORK WITH?

UH HUH.

I JUST WISH YOU'D HAVE DISCUSSIONS LIKE THAT WITH ME !!

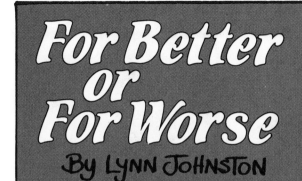

For Better or For Worse

By Lynn Johnston

GEE...

I HAVEN'T TALKED TO GRAMMA AND GRAMPA IN A LONG TIME!

HELLO, GRAMMA? IT'S ME—MICHAEL!

TELL HER ABOUT YOUR HOCKEY TOURNAMENT!

....UH....WE WON OUR HOCKEY TOURNAMENT.

THANK HER FOR THE SWEATER SHE SENT YOU.

THANKS FOR THE SWEATER YOU SENT ME.

TELL HER HOW YOU'RE DOING IN SCHOOL!

UM... I'M DOING FINE IN SCHOOL.

TELL HER THAT—

MOM—DO YOU WANNA TALK TO HER?

NO THANKS, DEAR... YOU'RE DOING FINE ALL BY YOURSELF!

For Better or For Worse

By Lynn Johnston

"RATTLE CLINK!"

OK—WHO TOOK MY KITCHEN SCISSORS?!!

THEY BELONG RIGHT HERE—AND EVERY TIME I NEED THEM— THEY'RE GONE!

I NEVER TOOK THEM!

I DUNNO WHERE THEY ARE!

THEY PROB'LY JUS DIST-APPEARED, MOM!

NOTHING CAN DISAPPEAR INTO THIN AIR, LIZZIE... —CAN IT, MOM?

NO....

JUST THE SCISSORS, SCOTCH TAPE, THE STAPLER, PENCILS BATH PLUG, PLIERS, SOCKS, CORKSCREW, THE EGG TIMER, MY THIMBLE, THE SCREWDRIVER, THE...

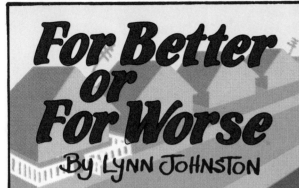

For Better or For Worse
By Lynn Johnston

SO LONG, GUYS...

MICHAEL... ISN'T ELIZABETH WITH YOU?

NO...UH...WE WERE PLAYING HIDE AN' SEEK—AND I DON'T KNOW WHERE SHE WENT!

I'VE CALLED ALL THE NEIGHBORS—AND NOBODY'S SEEN HER!!

I'M GOING TO WALK ALL OVER TOWN 'TILL I FIND HER!

WAIT, MOM—HERE'S ONE OF HER BOOTS...

ELIZABETH!—WHAT ARE YOU DOING UNDER THE SINK?

I PLAYING HIDE AN' SEEK ON MICHAEL!

...DID I WIN?

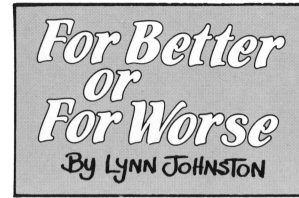

For Better or For Worse
By Lynn Johnston

MICHAEL, WILL YOU PLEASE DO YOUR DROOLING SOMEWHERE ELSE!

MOM, THERE'S A CHERRY IN THIS CAKE, HERE ... CAN I PULL IT OUT?

NO. YOU'VE HAD 2 PIECES. YOU CANNOT PULL OUT THAT CHERRY!

BUT, IT'S JUST STICKING OUT HERE AND...

I SAID NO!!!

OOPS.

POIT!

IT SORT OF FELL OUT. - CAN I HAVE IT?

FOR THE LAST TIME - NO!

62

For Better or For Worse
By Lynn Johnston

WASN'T THAT A LOVELY WEDDING, JOHN!

YEAH.... BROUGHT BACK MEMORIES OF OUR OWN!

WE HAD DAFFODILS IN THE CHURCH.... AND YOUR BROTHER MADE SUCH A FUNNY SPEECH LATER!

YESSIR—OUR RECEPTION WAS SOME PARTY!

WAS I THERE DADDY?

NO, YOU WEREN'T THERE, ELIZABETH!

WAS MICHAEL?

NO!!

HOWCOME?

OH, LIZZIE— YOU JUST WEREN'T— THAT'S ALL!

WE NEVER GET IMBITED TO ANYFING!!

For Better or For Worse

By Lynn Johnston

OW!

LOOK AT THIS, JOHN — I CAN STILL WORK A YO-YO!

HEY, LET ME TRY!

I WON A YO-YO ONCE FOR SINGING AT THE NEIGHBORHOOD THEATRE!

YEAH... SATURDAY MATINEES — A BOX OF POPCORN AND A CHEEK FULL OF JAW-BREAKERS!

REMEMBER HORSESHOE SUCKERS?

AND MISSION ORANGE IN THE BIG BROWN BOTTLES!

— AND SCRUB BASEBALL!

AND MARBLES! AND JACKS!

SEE, ELIZABETH... I **TOLD** YOU THEY WERE KIDS ONCE!!

For Better or For Worse By Lynn Johnston

I GOT A RED ONE!!

WE'D BETTER TIE THAT BALLOON TO YOUR WRIST, LIZZIE—OR IT WILL FLY AWAY!

NO! NO-WANNA! GONNA HOLD IT!!

IF YOU LET GO—YOU'LL LOSE IT—SO LET ME—

NO!

AAAAH!!

SOMETIMES YOU JUST CAN'T SAY "I TOLD YOU SO!"

For Better or For Worse

By Lynn Johnston

I DON'T KNOW WHAT'S SO GOOD ABOUT GROWNUP PARTIES....

ALL THEY DO IS TALK.

YACK! YACK!

GOSSIP TALK EAT MUNCH!

HI, THERE! WELL, THANKS, ELIZABETH.

YACK YACK

THAT'S, UH...INTERESTING STUFF, ELLY — ER, WHAT IS IT?

ELIZABETH!!

ECONO SIZE DOG KIBBLE

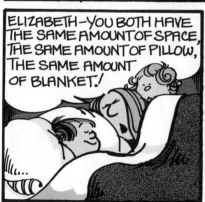

For Better or For Worse

By Lynn Johnston

I DON'T WANNA WALK ALL THE WAY TO THE CHANGING HOUSE, MOM.

I'M GONNA GET INTO MY BATHING SUIT 'WAY OVER HERE UNDER THIS BLANKET!

OK-I'M CHANGING — NOBODY'S GONNA SEE ME !!!

NOBODY CAN LOOK UNDER THIS BLANKET- 'CAUSE I'M CHANGING !!

I GOT MY CLOTHES OFF- BUT NOBODY CAN SEE UNDER THIS BLANKET!

NOBODY LOOK! - I'M JUST ABOUT READY TO PUT ON-

AAAAA AAAAA AGH!

I HATED TO DISAPPOINT HIM.